*Bob's Big Adventure is a story of hope, determination, and kindness. When Bob the Burro ran off into the desert mountains, his family had no idea the journey that was about to unfold and the friendships that would be created along the way. Being new to the community, Bob's family was unfamiliar with the area and those who lived there. But, that quickly changed as the community rallied together to bring Bob home. This book is dedicated to **everyone** who supported us and our journey.*

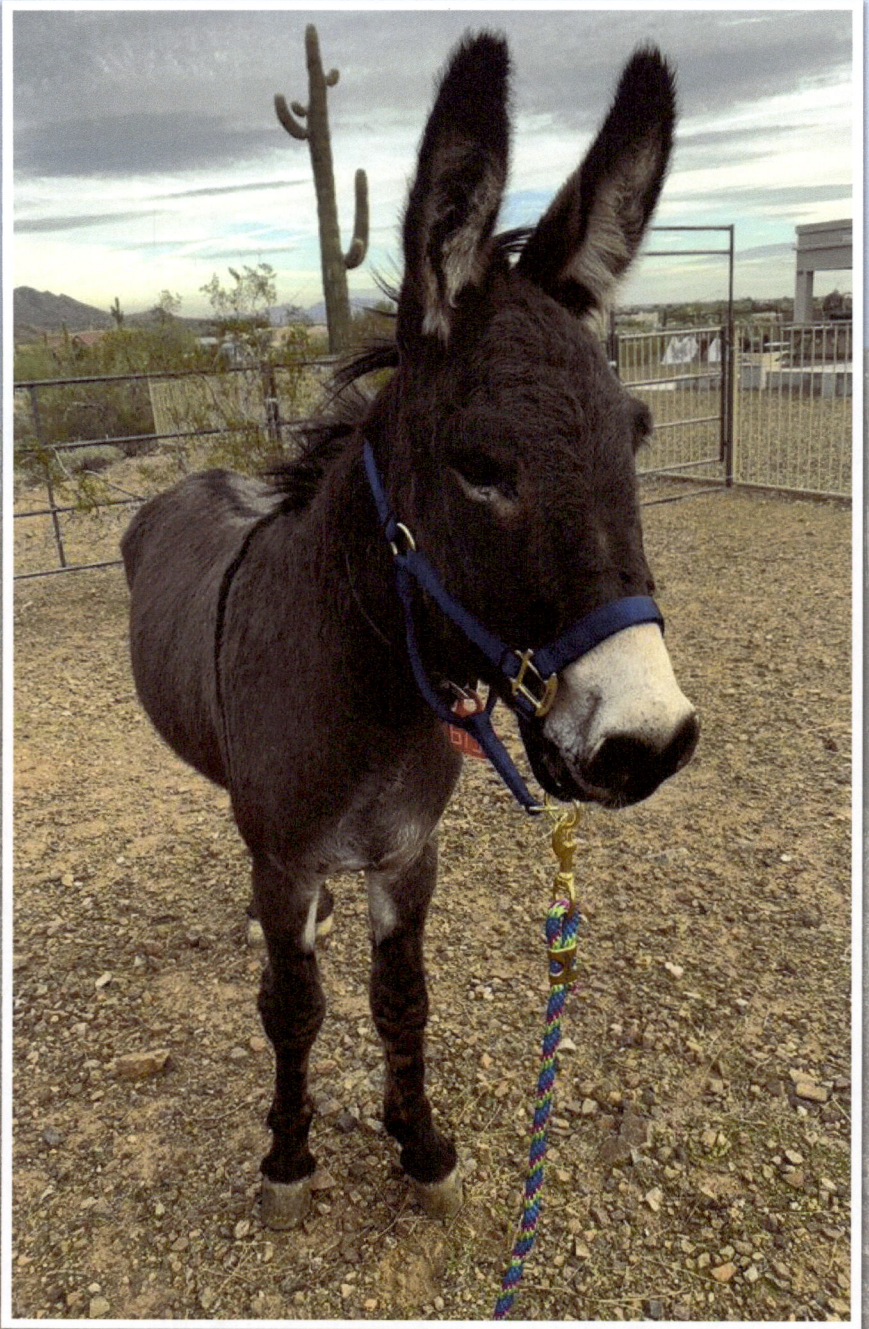

Bob's Big
Adventure

A true story of a teenager's
journey to find her lost pet burro

By: Lindsey Quine

Cover Illustration by: Patti C.

Produced by Connected Horizons, LLC

Revision 202109 | ISBN: 978-1-7326014-2-0

CONNECTED HORIZONS
BUSINESS • REAL ESTATE • INFORMATION TECHNOLOGY CONSULTANTS

My story started in February of 2021 when I walked out of the horse trailer and saw my family for the very first time. Ever since that day, they have called me Bob....Bob the Burro. I am originally from the Cibola-Trigo desert near Quartzite, Arizona. That desert is pretty boring; not much to see or experience except an occasional dirt bike, ATV (All- Terrain Vehicle), or UTV (Utility Terrain Vehicle). Many people say that us burros from the Cibola-Trigo desert are "as wild as they come".

I was about 5 years old when I was rounded up by the BLM (Bureau of Land Management). Food and water are becoming harder to find in the desert due to years of little rain, so some of us get to live with humans who help take care of us. As happy as I am to have food and water always available, I miss being free and roaming the open desert.

My family was so happy when I arrived. They worked with me everyday to help me get used to my new life. They taught me how to eat and drink out of these big buckets, how to walk on a lead rope, and how to gently eat treats by hand. Boy, I sure do love those treats! My family also spent a lot of time talking to me and petting me. At first, I wasn't sure why they kept doing all of these things, but after a few days I really started to like my family. Soon, I even found myself braying when I saw them coming (I bray when I'm excited and happy!).

Even though I liked my whole family, the younger girl of my family was my favorite. The family called her Lindsey. She would feed me, take me on walks in my pen, and help me calm down when I would get nervous or upset by something new. Lindsey really seemed to understand me.

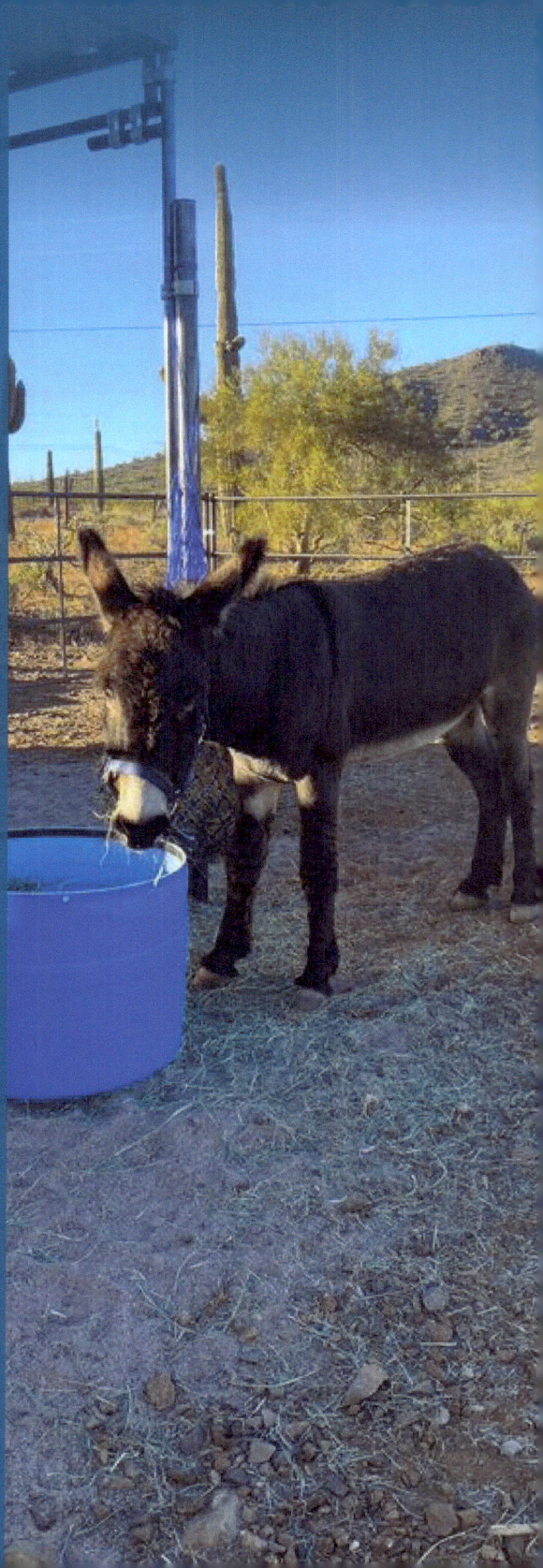

My family had a large pen for me to roam around in. My pen looked out into a desert mountain area where I would see coyotes, bobcats, deer, and many other desert animals. Inside my pen, there was plenty of dirt for me to roll around in and a little mesquite tree. I really liked the mesquite tree...so much so that I ate most of it within my first few weeks at my new home. Even though I was adjusting to my new home with my family, every day I would look off into the desert mountains behind my pen and think about being free. I knew a part of me was still wild.

After a few months of daily training, my family started to slowly take me out of my pen so I could have more space to practice walking on my lead rope. There was another fenced-in area next to my pen that we started to walk around in. My family would spend a lot of time in this area so I was excited to walk around and explore "their space".

The Day My Adventure Began

One morning, as Lindsey and I were walking around "their space," I found myself gazing off into the desert mountains, dreaming of being free again. I kept looking at Lindsey to try to get my mind

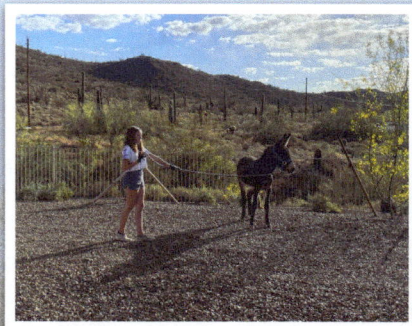

off the desert mountain, but I felt like it was just calling my name. As we started walking back to my pen, I heard an unfamiliar noise and got spooked (unfortunately, this happened often). The next thing I knew I was running up the mountain. My wild part had taken over.

As I ran into the desert mountain range, Lindsey and the dad followed me. I did not know what to do. As much as I had grown to love my family, the *wild* part of me was overpowering. I could hear Lindsey's calming tone and words echoing through the mountains, "Bob, please stop. You will be okay. Please come home." I often stopped running and let them get close to me, but then my instincts would take over and off I would run. I continued to run up and down the mountains all morning with my family (well, at least, the dad) close behind. I stayed on the mountains behind my family's home for most of the day, always keeping my family's home in sight. As much as I wanted to return, I also wanted to be free.

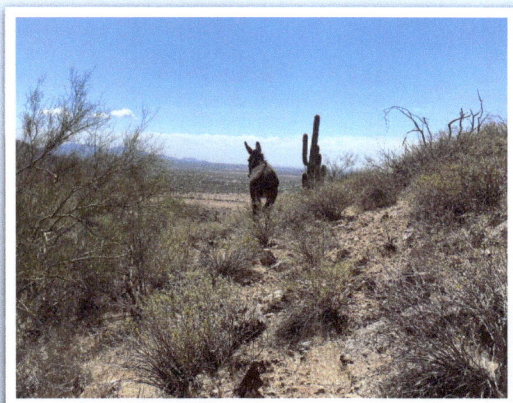

The dad finally stopped following me in the early afternoon. I found some shelter among the trees in a canyon on the other side of the mountain. As I rested, I heard horses coming up the mountain. It only took a few minutes to realize that these horses (and their riders) were searching for me. They spotted me in the canyon and started to run toward me. I began running, up the mountains and then back into the canyon, over and over with the horses right behind me. The horses started to slow down as I continued to run up and down the mountains. Eventually, the horses stopped and then left the canyon. Phew, that was tiring. I travelled back down into the canyon and found a tree to take a rest.

The sun was beginning to set. The day was ending and I thought that my adventures for the day were coming to an end as well. I thought wrong. All of a sudden, coming over the mountain and into the canyon was another horse. This horse was huge and the rider was swinging a rope. "Oh no, a roper!", I thought. The horse spotted me and the chase began. Up the mountain. Down the mountain. Over and over again with the horse right behind me. All of a sudden, I felt the rope around my head. Not my neck, but my head. I moved my head back, forth, up and down until the rope finally came loose. I was free! Off I ran, but this time, I did not hear the galloping of the horse behind me. When I reached the top of the mountain, I looked back and saw the horse leaving. Phew, I had outrun that horse as well.

As the sun set and the canyon slowly went dark, I found some grass and trees to eat before getting some rest for the night. What a day!

The First Week of My Adventure

The next few days were pretty quiet for me, but not for my family. As I roamed the desert mountains searching for food and water, my family was busy connecting with many wonderful people that wanted to help find me and bring me home. There was a lot of activity in the desert mountains that week from all of the connections my family had made. I saw more horseback riders (but they didn't chase me this time), donkey's with their owners, and hikers. I even saw this thing that looked like a little helicopter (humans call it a drone) flying in the air above me. Even though I saw them, it didn't seem like any of these things spotted me. But, all of this activity made it very clear that my family was not going to give up on bringing me home.

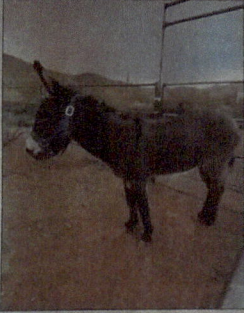

LOST PET BURRO

- Dark gray BLM rescued burro
- Has on a blue halter and rainbow lead rope
- Got loose on Sunday, April 18th
- SPOOKS EASILY

DO NOT CHASE OR APPROACH

CALL or TEXT if seen or with any info

HARTT is assisting (azhartt.org)

My family also got in touch with some really amazing people from an organization called HARTT (Humane Animal Rescue and Trapping Team). "HARTT is a volunteer-based Arizona nonprofit organization that humanely captures lost family pets, homeless dogs, and homeless cats who are severely injured. Typically, these animals cannot easily be leashed, picked up or captured through ordinary means. Bringing these animals to safety often requires extraordinary patience, specialized strategy, skill and equipment, as well as time and resources." (http://azhartt.org). Although HARTT had never been involved in a "burro rescue", volunteers Patti and Gary enthusiastically agreed to lead the "Bring Bob Home" team and immediately started to post flyers about Bob all over the area.

Water Source Found

After a few days of wandering the desert mountains, I found some water a few miles from where my adventure first started. The water source was located in a low lying wash between the mountains. It was protected by overgrown trees and brush. The terrain near my water source was very rocky and steep. The natural spring water was contained in a trough covered in algae that gave the water a nice sweet taste. I knew that this would need to be my source of water as I continued on my adventure.

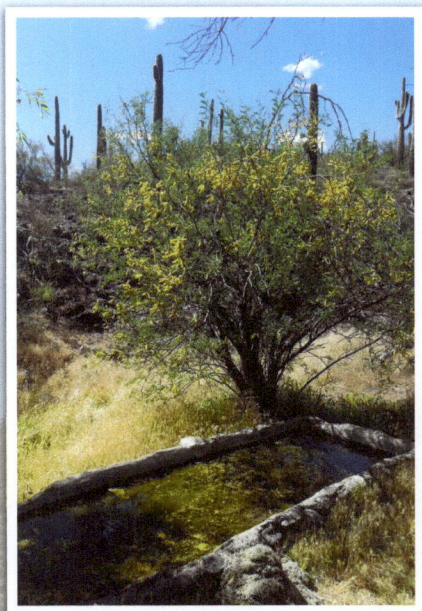

I was relieved to find water and started to explore the mountain area near my water source. I found areas with lots of bermuda grass and mesquite trees to eat. I spent many days on the mountainside under a tree getting familiar with the area. There was a street not too far from the mountain but there wasn't much traffic (at first). There were hiking trails that were frequented by hikers on foot and on horse. Overall, it was a very quiet area that seemed safe and protected.

Day 6 of My Adventure

At the end of the first week, I heard a voice that sounded familiar. I looked down the mountain and saw a lady with Lindsey and the mom from my family. The lady was guiding them down into the wash near my water source. As I watched them, I could hear her say that this is the only known water source for many miles. They hiked around the area for a bit and then the lady noticed signs that I had been there. She spotted my poop and a trail in the dirt made by my lead rope. While these could be signs of other animals, Lindsey knew that these were signs that I had been there. Little did she know that I was still there.

Day 7 of My Adventure

One week later, my family continued to look for me. The dad hiked many miles up and down the steep mountain terrain behind the family house. It was the same area that he and I walked the day I got loose. As hopeful as he was that I was still in that area, I had moved on so he did not see me. A few miles north of the family home, Lindsey and the mom hiked the backside of the desert mountain area as well as a trail that led to a local cow ranch where there was plenty of water. Although I initially travelled north, I then went to the east toward my water source, so they did not find me either.

After hiking for many hours in the heat, my family decided to drive up the road near my water source. As they were heading back down the mountain toward home, I noticed a truck come to an abrupt stop in the middle of the road. I was standing on the side of the mountain under a tree, trying to get some relief from the hot sun. I slowly backed up to get farther behind the tree, but it was too late. I noticed them looking straight toward me. Then I heard Lindsey's voice, "Bob...is that you?". I had been spotted.

A little while later, the lady who helped Lindsey and the mom discover my water source came. The lady started hiking up the mountain toward me. What was she going to do? I got scared and started moving away from her, farther up the mountain. Eventually, she stopped pursuing me and returned to the street with the other people. By now, my family's truck had left and returned with another truck too. On the back of

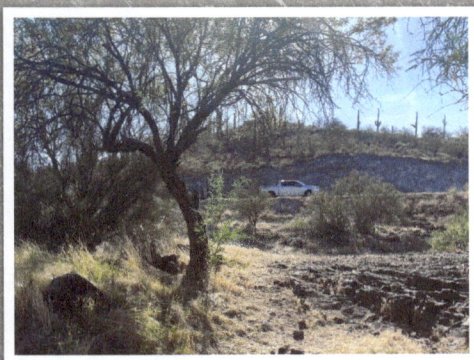

my family's truck was a trailer with horse panels, just like the ones at my home and the ones in the desert where I was originally captured. I watched as my family and the people from the other truck (who I later learned were Gary and Patti from HARTT) carefully carried the panels down the hill and into a flat, grassy clearing in the valley. They arranged the panels into an open pen, put up some boxes on trees (I later learned that these boxes were actually cameras), and put some water and treats inside the pen area. Although I was curious about what they were doing, my fear kept me a safe distance away from the pen, water, treats, and.... cameras.

I had been spotted by my family. Seeing them brought many mixed feelings; I really miss them but I also love being free in the desert. Unsure of what to do next, I stayed on my same nightly routine of eating and getting water from my usual water source.

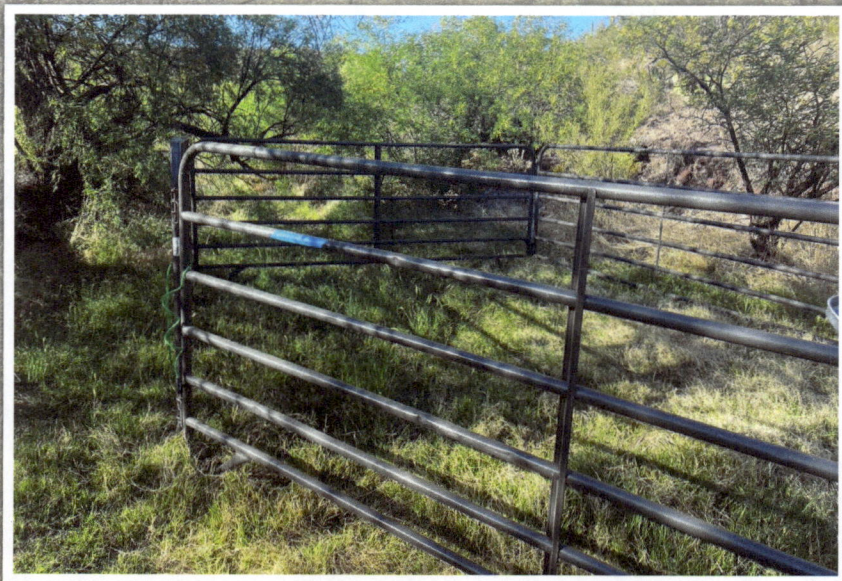

Day 8 of My Adventure

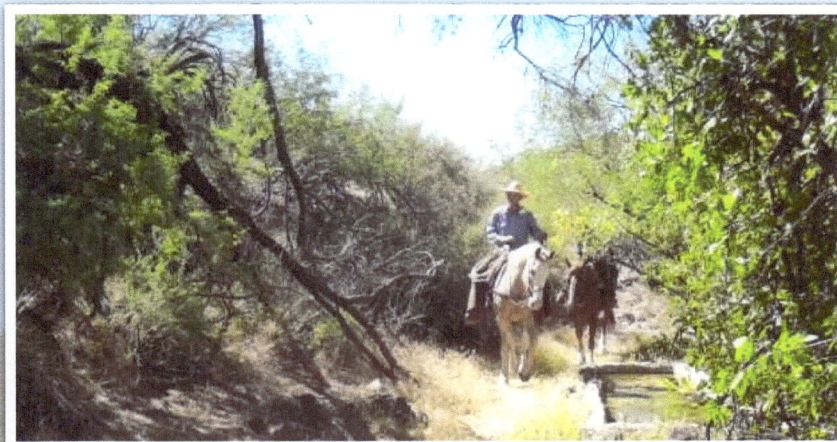

When the sun rose, I headed out on my normal walk through the wash, mountains, and valley's. But this time, something was very different. I noticed a lot of hikers and horses with riders. There were also ATV's, UTV's, dirt bikes, and motorcycles around the area and even on the mountain trails. They all seemed to be looking for something or someone.

As I carefully travelled through the desert mountain, trying not to be seen, I found myself veering off my normal path in order to avoid people. This brought me closer to houses and the nearby street. It was then that I noticed a sign with what looked like a picture of me. "Oh my, they are all looking for ME!", I thought.

The increase in foot, horse, and vehicle traffic made me very nervous. At one point, I was being chased by a dirt bike while people were walking toward me. I ran to try to get away and ended up in the middle of the street looking straight into the eyes of the driver of a moving car. The driver slammed on his brakes and I quickly ran back into the desert mountains.

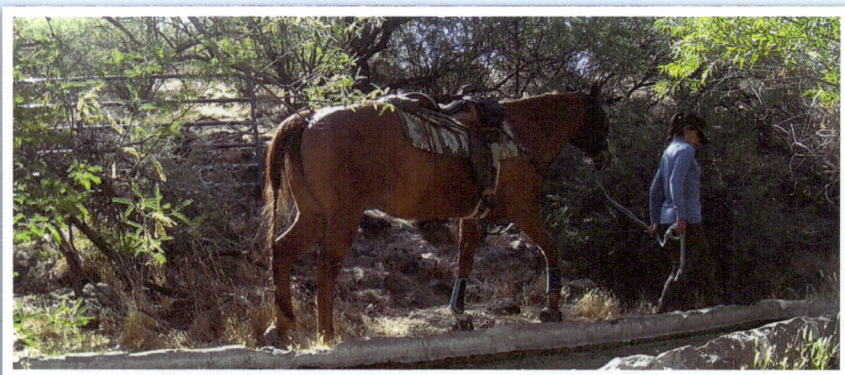

Many people saw me today and called my family to let them know where I had been sighted. Later in the day, things seemed to calm down so I ventured out of the valley where I had found safety and protection in the desert shrubs. I started to walk up the mountain where I could get a better look at the area to see if more people were going to come look for me. For the first time today, it was quiet and peaceful again.

As the sun started to set, a truck with a horse trailer came into the area. This time though, a donkey was brought out of the trailer. A lady started to walk with the donkey up the road and into the desert mountain area right below where I was standing under a tree on the side of the mountain. I then noticed my family up on the nearby road watching the lady and her donkey as they started to hike the mountain toward me.

The lady is called Rachel and she brought her donkey, Freya, to help get me home. Rachel is the owner of Starbird, a donkey who got loose and went on a very long adventure in the Sonoran Desert. Rachel was determined to bring Starbird home. Finally after 6 months of tracking her, she was able to capture her and bring her home safely. Rachel shared her experience with Starbird and gave my family a lot of information, suggestions, ideas, and hope on how to capture me. But, I am still not sure I am ready to be captured yet.

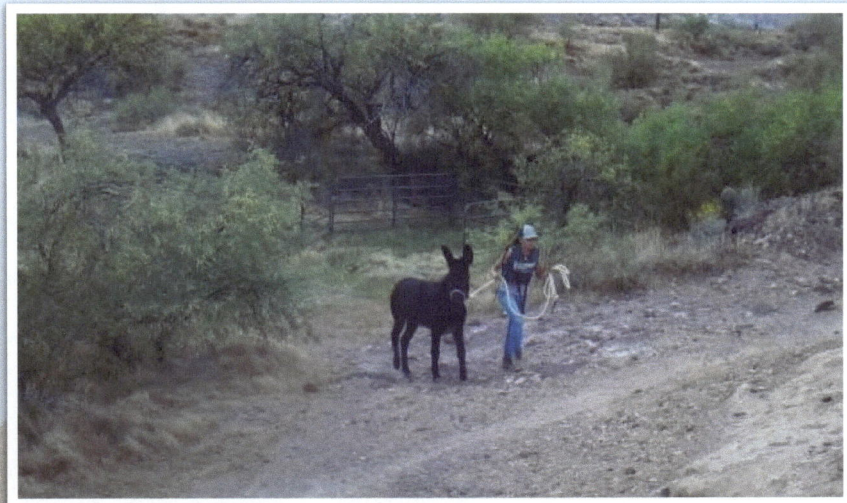

As Rachel and Freya hiked the mountain closer to me, I got scared and ran off. I started to run slowly, still watching their every move. Freya then brayed (the sound a donkey makes to communicate to others), but that made me even more scared so I ran over the top of the mountain. I could not be seen anymore. Rachel and Freya eventually started walking back toward the road. I stayed hidden as I could still hear Rachel and my family talking. When it was quiet again, I walked to the top of the mountain so I could see that everyone had left. It was getting dark and I felt relieved that this day was finally over.

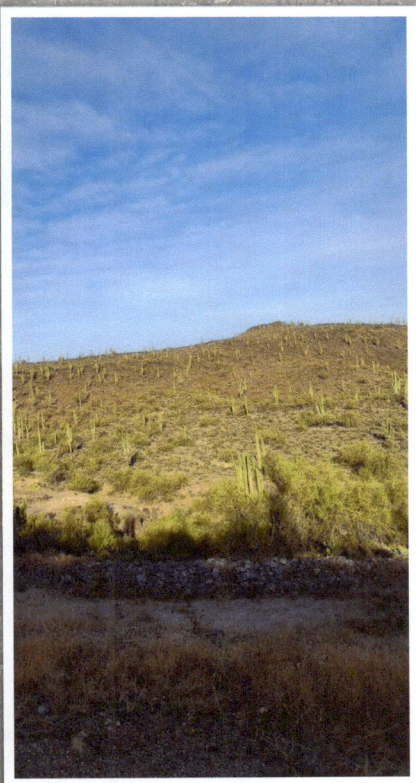

Week 2 of My Adventure

Over the next few days, I tried to stay quiet and hidden during the daylight. I knew that many people were looking for me but I wasn't ready for my adventure to be over yet. I frequented my water source only at night to avoid being seen. I noticed that the boxes (cameras) that were placed near the pen in the open grassy area were now on the trees near my water source.

It was May in Arizona and the days were getting hotter. I needed water more frequently so that I would have enough energy to keep moving during the day. Eventually, I was caught on camera getting a drink and walking around the area by the water trough. I realized I had been caught on camera when my family, Gary, and Patti started to come and check the boxes (cameras) on the trees every day.

A few days after they saw me on camera by the water trough, my family, Gary, and Patti moved the horse panels. The panels were still in the open grassy area close to where they first saw me on the mountain side. They carried the panels, one by one up and down the rocky steep trail near the water trough. At first, they arranged the panels and created a small, open pen next to the water trough.

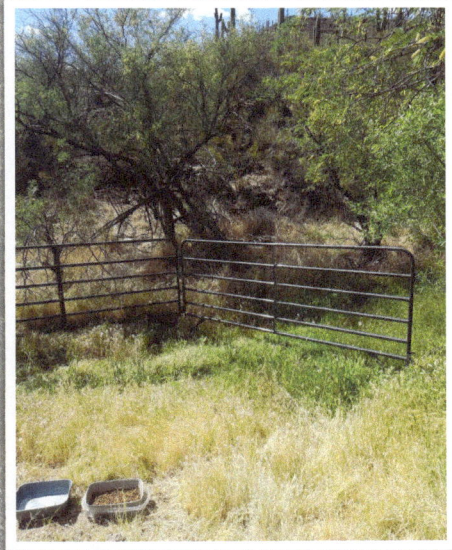

A few days later, they moved the panels again and arranged them behind the water trough. They stayed in that area for a while, but more panels were added to make the pen larger. Every time they moved the panels they left me special treats and food. Although I didn't understand why they kept moving the panels, I knew when things were different and I tried to stay far away from the panels. But, on occasion, I was brave and went near the pen to get a carrot or special food that they left...but that wasn't too often.

Week 3 and 4 of My Adventure

Over the next couple of weeks, we all seemed to be adjusting to our new routine. Every morning, Gary and Patti would come to my water source and check some of the camera's (remove and replace the memory cards). My family would also come in the morning to check the other cameras. Right before dusk, my family, Gary, and Patti would come back to my water source, talk, move things around, and leave.

Since my family, Gary, and Patti came to my water source during the day, I continued my same daily routine by walking my same path around the mountains and into the valley's. I loved to graze on all of the trees and fresh grass. I would often find a bush or tree to lie under to try to stay cool from the hot afternoon sun.

In my travels, I discovered a very lush grassy area close to my water source. There was plenty of bermuda grass (my favorite) as well as Palo Verde trees and other shrubs in this area. Soon, I made this area part of my evening routine. Sometimes, I would go to the water source and get a drink and then come and hang out in this grassy area for a while and then go back to my water source.

My family, Gary, and Patti must have seen some "evidence" (poop) that I had been hanging out here because soon lots of cameras were there and some special treats for me. I didn't realize it at the time, but I guess I had left a lot of "evidence" there because my family, Gary, and Patti called that area, "Poop Palace."

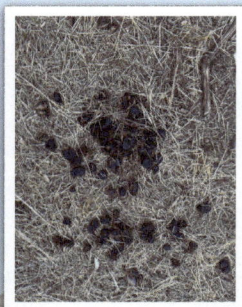

As my journey continued, I noticed that this desert area was very different from my first home (the one where I roamed before I was caught by the BLM). In addition to all of the mountains and valleys (my first home was pretty flat), this area had many other types of animal friends. As I walked (during the day and night), I met some deer, rabbits, bobcats, javelina, and coyotes. One

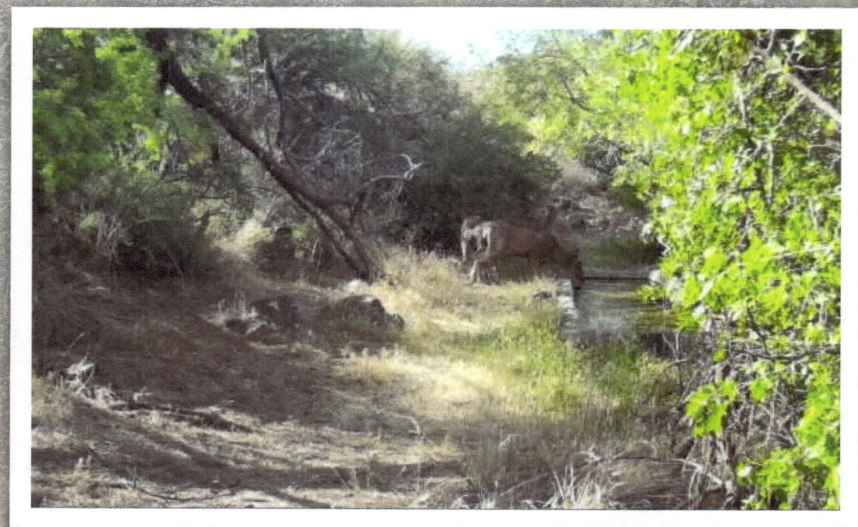

morning, from afar, I spotted a mountain lion at my water source. I tried to stay away from him. No matter how far I walked during the day, I would always find my way back to my water source.

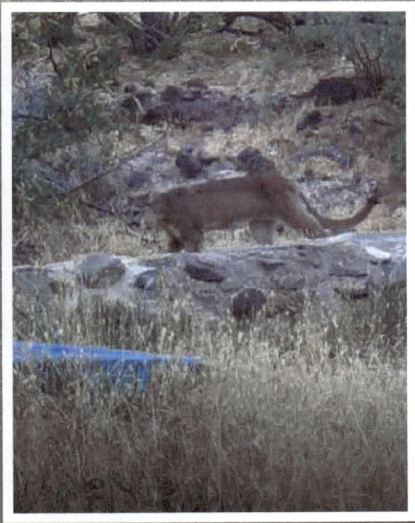

At first, I needed water every other day. But, as the Arizona summer heat became more intense, I found myself needing water more often. So, I started going to my water source every day. I also realized that as the days got hotter, the food I was eating in the desert wasn't tasting as good or filling me up as much. I have to admit, I started thinking about my life at home with my family more often.

During the weeks I walked my daily loop, I noticed a lot of people stopping by my water source. Some were on horseback while others were hiking. This time, they were not trying to catch me or chase me. They would stop at those cameras on the trees and talk to them. They would say things like, "I hope you find Bob soon" and "Good luck catching Bob." Wow, it seemed that everyone knew about me.

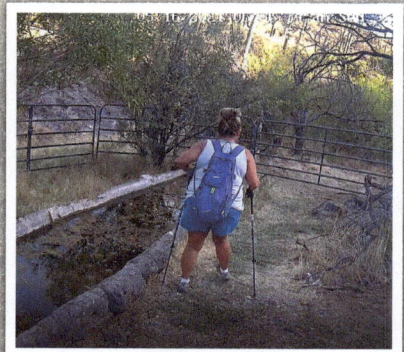

The Last Week of My Adventure

I had been on my own for 28 days. As much as I loved being free, independent, and "wild", I was also tired and lonely. I pretty much did the same thing every day by now. Walking my usual trail and trying to find food and shade from the afternoon sun.

One day, while on my daily walk, I heard loud noises coming from my water source. I went to the top of the mountain so I could see what was going on. It was my family, Gary, and Patti. Rachel was back too. They had more horse panels and they started carrying the panels down the steep and rocky mountain to my water source. I could not see what they were doing with the extra panels from the mountain top, so that night I went down to my water source to check it out.

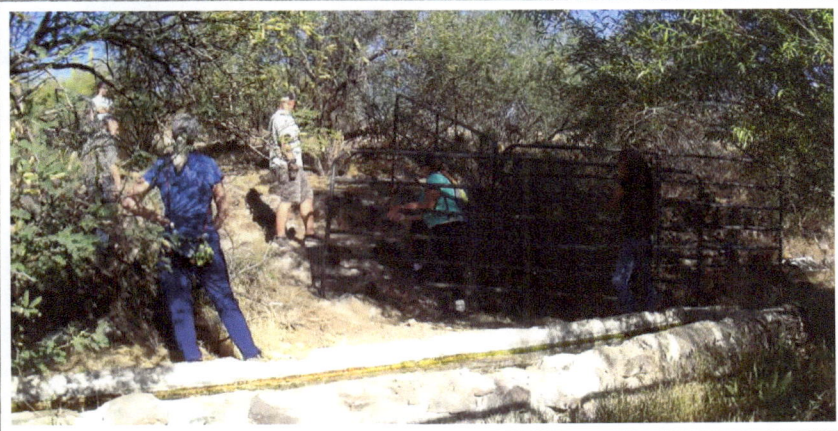

There were panels everywhere;
they were all around my water
source with three large openings
that I could walk through, but
I was scared. It was hot. I was
thirsty. I needed water. I walked
close to the panels to check them
out. I sniffed around and listened
for any sounds of concern. I
slowly checked out all three of
the openings, one by one, until I
was back at the top of the rocky
trail.

As you can probably tell by now, I get scared pretty easily.
Anything new or different scares me. Unfamiliar or loud noises
scare me. Quick or unexpected movements scare me. So, walking
near the new panels that were arranged close to the water trough
with defined openings was very scary.

Standing at the panel opening on my usual path, I sniffed the
opening again, took a deep breath, and bravely walked through the
opening to get a drink. I did it!

Having conquered my fear, I continued on with my daily routine... walking the same path everyday, grazing in the same grassy area and napping under the trees in the brush covered valley. Every evening, I would return to my water source. Over the next few days, I noticed changes near my water source. First, one of the openings that I really didn't use that often was closed. Oh well, I will just go to the water my usual way...down the rocky hill. After a few more days, another one of the openings in the panels was closed. Although I sometimes liked to use this path, the rocky hill was still my favorite and I guess now, it's my only way to my water.

As the panels were changing and closing, I began to realize that my family was slowly creating a pen just like my pen at my family's house. They even started to bring me some really delicious alfalfa hay. This tasted so good, especially since most of the food I was eating in the desert mountains was dried up, tasteless, and lacked nutrients.

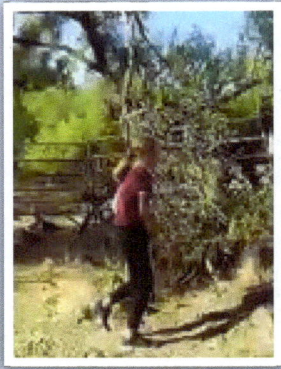

One day as I was walking my normal daytime path, I heard my family down by the water. I stopped on the top of the nearby mountain where I could see them. Lindsey was running from my water source up the rocky hill, over and over again. I could hear Patti say my name, "Be Bob...Be Bob." What on earth were they up to now? Little did I know that they were timing Lindsey to see how fast she could get up the rocky hill from the water. Still unsure why they were doing this, I was impressed with Lindsey's speed up the rocky hill (but she definitely wasn't as fast as me.).

A day later, when I went to the water trough, I noticed another big change. There was this little structure (a tent) covered with fake leaves next to the pen. I knew they were fake because I smelled them to see if I could eat them and they did not smell like leaves at all. I walked around

sniffing the structure, but it didn't seem too important to me.

Before I knew it, there was another change near my water source. My main path to the water got really narrow and looked different. There was now a bar over my head and extra metal chained to one of the panel's. It looked similar to the gate that was in my pen at my family's house. I was really reluctant to walk through "the gate". I walked around to the other sides of the panels but nothing else was open. The days were getting really hot and I was thirsty. So, I went back to "the gate", sniffed around it, nudged it with my nose, and then walked through it. Everything seemed fine so I went and enjoyed some water and alfalfa and then left through "the gate".

The next day, I heard some unfamiliar voices with my family, Gary, and Patti. I went to the top of the mountain where I could watch and listen without being seen. The large group of people walked from my water source down the path to my grassy hangout place (Poop Palace).The people talked a lot and then came back to my water source. The group hiked up and down the mountains around my water source. It sounded like they were coming up with a plan to get me home.

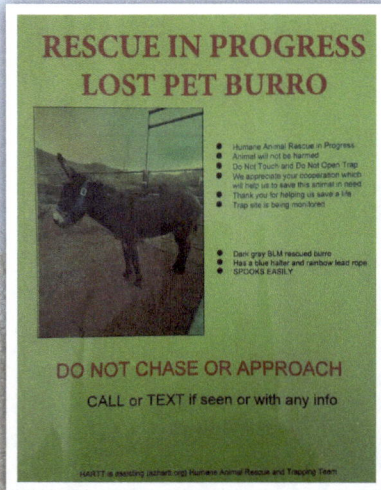

RESCUE IN PROGRESS
LOST PET BURRO

- Humane Animal Rescue in Progress
- Animal will not be harmed
- Do Not Touch and Do Not Open Trap
- We appreciate your cooperation which will help us to save this animal in need
- Thank you for helping us save a life
- Trap site is being monitored

- Dark gray BLM rescued burro
- Has a blue halter and rainbow lead rope
- SPOOKS EASILY

DO NOT CHASE OR APPROACH
CALL or TEXT if seen or with any info

HARTT is assisting (azhartt.org) Humane Animal Rescue and Trapping Team

I heard them talk about three plans. Plan A was to use more panels to create a chute that I would walk/run through as I climbed the steep and rocky mountain out of the wash up to an awaiting trailer. Plan B was to sedate me, secure me to a board, and then pull me up the mountain with a pulley system attached to a truck or UTV. Plan C was to sedate me and then place me in a helicopter rescue basket and fly me home. By the sounds of it, I knew my adventure was coming to an end.

I had very mixed feelings about going home. I missed the safety and security of my pen, daily food and water, and the love and attention from my family. But, when I was home, I missed my freedom and being in the wild.

That night, there was a lot of unfamiliar "people noises" in the desert mountains (loud voices, gunshots, loud and fast cars, etc.). I was not sure if it was safe to go to the water, so I decided to stay safe and hide under a tree in a small valley for the night. What I didn't know at the time was that my family, Gary, and Patti were ready to catch me that night. The dad was in that cloth structure (tent) by my water source while Lindsey, the mom, and Gary were waiting up the road and out of sight. Patti was at home watching the live camera positioned by my water source. Lindsey's older sister was at home ready to be the communication organizer since there was very limited cell service at the water source. They waited until 3 a.m. for me to come and get a drink before calling it a night.

Back at the family home, my family rested a bit and then decided to try to catch me again that night. Since I didn't get any water last night, they knew I would need some water tonight. They contacted Gary and Patti who agreed with the plan. "Operation Catch Bob, Night 2" was set.

Capture Night

At about 7pm, my family, Gary, and Patti arrived at my water source. After checking to make sure all of the panels were secure, testing the gate closure system, and freshening up the alfalfa, the dad went into the cloth structure (tent) and Lindsey, the mom, and Gary went up the hill and out of sight. Patti went home to watch the live camera by my water source and Lindsey's sister was ready at home to make the necessary calls.

Even though I usually wait until about midnight to get water, I decided to start heading to my water source around nightfall. Since I didn't get a drink last night, I was extra thirsty tonight. As soon as the sun went down I started to scope out the area to make sure it was safe. I walked around the structure (tent) and around the outside of the panels near my water source. Everything seemed fine, but I wanted to wait until it got a little darker. About an hour later, I headed down to the water.

05/23/2021 09:47:32 pm SUN

As I went to get a drink, I heard a noise. I quickly turned around and realized that the noise I heard was the closing of the gate. I was stuck. I walked up the rocky hill and used my head to try to nudge the gate open. It was locked shut.

What I later learned is that Gary had created a remote enabled gate closing system. The dad had the remote for the gate in the structure (tent). When I put my head down to take a drink, he pushed the button on the remote which demagnetized the gate causing it to slam shut and lock. Pure genius!

05/23/2021 09:48:07 pm SUN

After a few minutes, the dad came out of the structure (tent) and started to talk to me. I honestly don't remember what he was saying as I was overwhelmed by the smell of lavender oil. It was recommended to my family to use lavender oil to help calm me after I was contained. Many donkeys have tried to break through the panels by ramming into them after they are caught. Given my extreme fear of things, everyone was convinced that I would engage in this behavior. The lavender oil was to keep me as calm as possible so I did not get hurt. Well, as the dad was opening the bottle of lavender oil, it spilled all over him. So, the calming aroma of the dad as well as his familiar and calming voice helped me to remain calm. I paced around the pen and repeatedly snorted my displeasure. Lindsey then came down the mountain to where I was caught. Although she was talking to me, reassuring me, and offering me carrots, I was more interested in the voices coming from the road. What was going to happen next?

I heard the mom, dad, Gary, and Patti talking on the road. It seemed that the team that would help get me home would arrive in the morning. Lindsey was encouraging me to stay calm. I continued to pace and snort. I was scared...actually, I was terrified! I smelled the dad coming back down the mountain. The dad talked to me a little longer and then went back to the structure (tent). He said he was going to try to sleep for a bit. I am now trapped and alone. What should I do?

A few minutes later, I saw lights coming from the road. "Now what?", I thought. I started to pace around the pen again. I was so nervous. I heard car doors slam shut and then a new but familiar voice saying, "let's do this!" More footsteps started coming down the mountain. The new but familiar voice (Soleil) approached me. She knew my name and told me what a good boy I am. She quickly realized that I didn't like the headlamps and flashlights that were being used. It takes my eyes a long time to adjust from dark to light, so I feel blinded and scared. She told everyone to turn off their lights. Thankfully it was a full moon, so I could still see everyone and everything going on by the moonlight. She sang as she talked and gave me the reassurance that everything would be okay. As much as I had a hard time believing her, I also found comfort in her words. I don't know why, but I really liked this lady, Soleil.

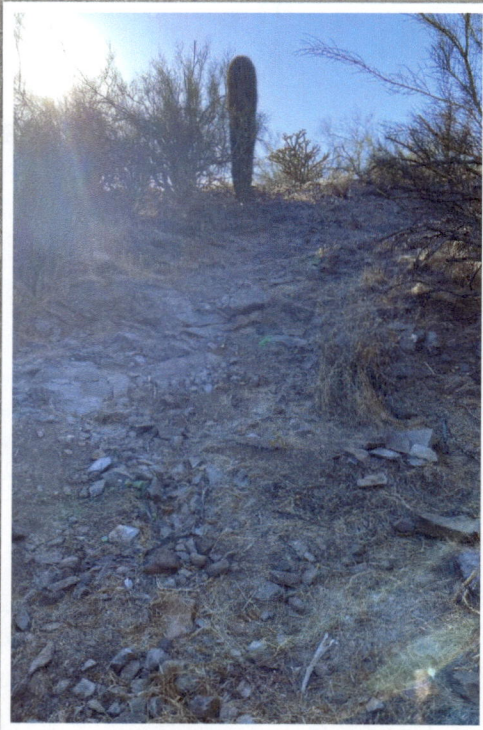

After she walked away, I heard a lot of clinking and clanking. I then saw my family and Gary bring down more and more panels...12 more to be exact. As the panels were brought down the mountain, Soleil guided them into position. They created a chute about 4 feet wide from my catch pen in the wash, up the mountain side. Plan A! They quickly secured the panels together and then opened one of the panels from my pen to lead me into the chute. Although I didn't know where the chute was taking me, I was nudged to move into the chute. The terrain was steep so I ran up the side of the mountain in the chute. At the top, another pen was waiting for me. This one was much smaller. As they started to close the panel to contain me in this smaller pen, I got scared and ran back down the mountain to my water source catch pen.

After a few minutes, everyone (including me) was calm and ready to try again. I ran back up the mountain in the chute to the smaller pen. This time, I saw Lindsey standing near the pen. I focused on Lindsey while Soleil closed the panel. I was caught in this smaller pen. They kept me there and started to move the panels from the chute. This time they took the panels farther up the mountain. It looked like they were attaching them to a horse trailer. They made another chute from the trailer down the mountain to another slightly flat area. The smaller holding pen, where I was contained, was very far away (at least 150 feet) from this chute. How were they going to get me there?

While I watched them moving the panels, Lindsey stayed with me. As she talked to me, she tried offering me carrots again (my favorite treat). Although I refused the carrots at first, her reassuring voice made me think back to being home with her and my family and without even thinking, I ate the carrot, then another, and then another.

Soleil, the mom, the dad, Patti, and Gary then returned to the holding pen. Soleil explained the next phase and how they were going to get me to the next chute. Each member of the team was going to pick up a corner of my smaller holding pen and then move the pen with me inside of it. What? This sounded like a crazy idea.

Soleil guided the process and within seconds I found myself walking inside the moving holding pen up the mountain toward the next chute. When we arrived at the next chute, one corner of the holding pen was opened and I was released into the chute that led to the trailer. Uh oh. Another new and unfamiliar experience. I was scared. I started walking up the chute toward the trailer, but as I got closer to the trailer, my fear took over and I stopped. I walked back into the holding pen, away from the trailer. Soleil then got in the pen with me. She started talking and singing to me again. She took what was left of my lead rope and gently guided me toward the trailer. Lindsey was standing at the trailer door encouraging me to walk toward her. I knew that once I was in the trailer I would be taken home. I decided that being in the wild was not meant for me...it was time to go home. With that in mind, I walked into the horse trailer and the doors closed behind me.

While I stood in the trailer and waited to leave, I thought about going home. I missed my family, my pen, my safety, my constant food and water, and, most of all, their love! We drove to my house. The trailer was backed up right to my pen, the doors opened and I walked into my pen. I was home. My 5 week adventure was officially over.

Although a part of me will always be "wild", this big adventure has made me realize that life really is better with my family. I love my family and I know that they love me because they spent 35 days working hard to bring me home. I know that my home is where I am supposed to be.

Acknowledgements

This story would not have been possible without the generous support of countless individuals both known and unknown. The author would like to give special recognition to the following organizations and individuals who without their support Bob would not have made it home.

- Arizona Equine Rescue Organization (AERO) - https://azequinerescue.org/
- Humane Animal Rescue and Trapping Team (HARTT) - https://azhartt.org/
- Brian S. - Drone Operator

The author would like to thank the following individuals for sharing their personal photographs to help bring this story to life.

- Gary and Patti C Family Photo Collection
- Mitra
- David and Amanda Quine Family Photo Collection

To Kathy

Thank you so much for reaching out to us and sharing your knowledge of the area. If you had not told us about the water source, we would have never found Bob. Your helpful information and tracking skills helped us realize Bob was in the area. Thank you so much for your help. - Lindsey Quine

To Rachel

Thank you so much for sharing all of your information and experience. You were so incredibly helpful in bringing Bob home. You gave us hope and encouragement when we needed it the most. You were so helpful in creating the catch pen and moving panels while always making sure that Bob would be safe. It was so nice to talk with someone who went through the same experience. Thank you so much for all of your help.- Lindsey Quine

To Patti and Gary (HARTT)

I don't even know how to thank you enough. Your endless hours spent working on getting Bob home was amazing and so appreciated. You both did so much to help locate, capture, and bring Bob home; from making daily trips to the trough to check camera footage, change batteries, rearrange camera locations, carry panels up and down the steep and rugged terrain to inventing a remote control gate closing system, hanging dozens of flyers, and so much more. You even stayed up all night with us on both capture night 1 and 2. None of this would have been possible without you both. Thank you so much for never giving up and helping us through the wild adventure. - Lindsey Quine

To Soleil (AERO)

Thank you so much for your help, support, and expertise. Without you, we would have never gotten Bob home. At first, I was very hesitant and worried with your idea of having Bob run up the chute. I put a lot of faith in you and I am so glad I trusted you during the whole experience. We did what I never thought was possible because of you. And, I especially loved your calming singing voice. "Moving Burro's at Midnight" will always hold a special place in my heart. Thank you so much for your help in bringing Bob home - Lindsey Quine

www.ingramcontent.com/pod-product-compliance
Lightning Source LLC
Chambersburg PA
CBHW041227270326
41934CB00001B/25